PAUL JAMES CULSHAW

# TELL ME WHAT YOU SEE

Published in 2024
Hidden Voice Publishing
Find us on Facebook
Edited: Joel Sadler-Puckering
Produced by: Anthony Sadler-Puckering

TELL ME WHAT YOU SEE
copyright © Paul James Culshaw

Cover Art By: Paul James Culshaw

# *INTRODUCTION*

One of my Primary School teachers once told me Mam and Dad: "Paul will be fine because he will be able to blag his way through life". So far so good, I think.

I have been very lucky to grow up with loving, supportive parents, family and friends. No expectations but experiences I will always be grateful for.

I have shared some of the most beautiful highs and gone through sadness that words can't express. Everything we go through, good or bad can in some way always help us grow and evolve.

The opportunity to work with my best friend on this project was one I jumped at the chance to do. The stars aligned all those years ago for us to find each other, and they keep reminding us of that from time to time. We never forget to listen to those stars.

I really hope this book, the photos and the poems help find a connection for whoever reads it.

Never too old to learn.
Never too young to start listening.
Try to feel the beauty others might not see in life.
Be kind. Be honest. Be you. Always.

For me beautiful Dad. I miss you every single day, but I love you forever.

# FOREWORD

I suppose, like many things in my life, creating this book has been a little unconventional and initially spontaneous. I think one of the blissful things about getting older, is learning that everything you do takes as much time as is needed. I have been very lucky to be able to share the ideas that just pop into my head, with soul mates who not only know me and how I think, but who also have their own amazing, unique passions and ideas too.

Partly this led me to start taking photos. Always trying to improve on my skills with the camera, and my connection to how I feel when I see things in the world is ever changing. The phrase 'a picture speaks a thousand words' grabbed me when focussing on this project. How cool that capturing moments and combining them with how others see them, can lead to hearing them tell how they feel about them? That is a beauty within itself. How others can express how they see and what they feel, from photos I've captured.

One of the most exciting prospects from this book is, discovering what YOU see…

Look again. Tell me what you see.

*Paul James Culshaw. Photographer.*

# CONTENTS
## *TELL ME WHAT YOU SEE*

**PAUL JAMES CULSHAW**
*WAIT* — 13

**ANTHONY SADLER-PUCKERING**
*JUST ONE CANDLE MORE* — 15

**MARIA BYRNE**
*SOMETIMES* — 17

**JENNIFER TYSON**
*EAST WINDS* — 18

**SARAH PRITCHARD**
*SERENITY* — 21

**EMMA HULANCE**
*BLACK BERETS* — 23

**JOEL SADLER-PUCKERING**
*THEY BUILT THIS PLACE* — 25

**KATIE HAIGH**
*PAINTINGS BY NATURE* — 27

**CAROLYNNE NELSON** — 29
*IT WON'T BE FOREVER*

**PAUL JAMES CULSHAW** — 31
*BOUND IMAGER*

# TELL ME WHAT YOU SEE

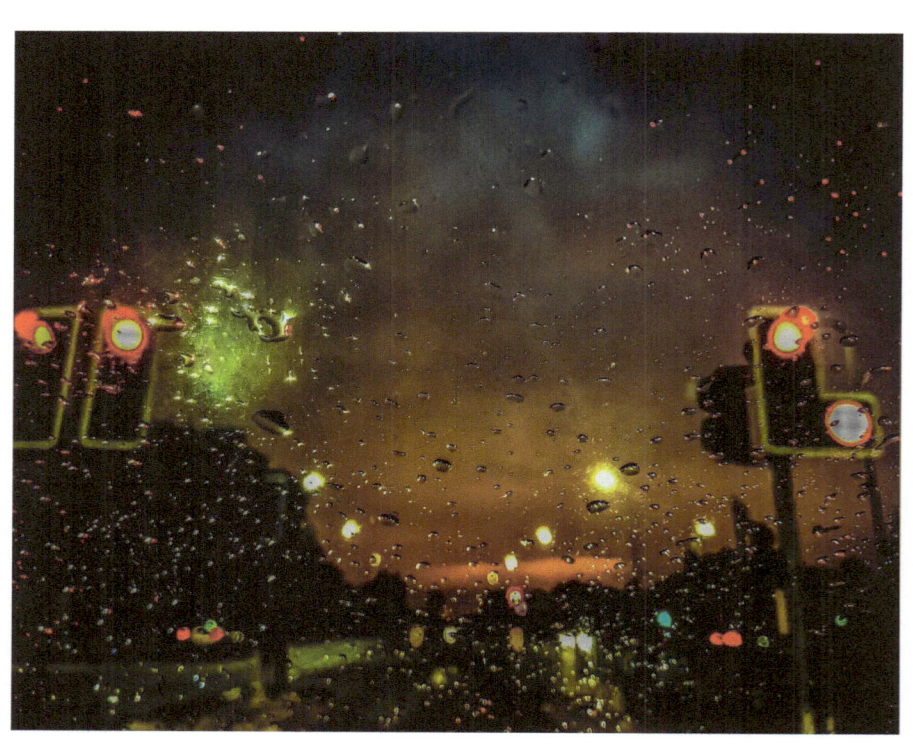

# PAUL JAMES CULSHAW

## *WAIT*

That moment. To pause. Wait.
Travelling from one place to the other.
From A to B and back again.
The colour says Stop! Wait.
Listen to the rain fall on the glass.
Breathe.
Where have I just been?
Where am I going?
The streetlights line up, in uniform, guiding the way.
Not yet, wait.
Droplets on the window are still and clear.
They won't move until it's time to - or forced.
A chance to focus through the blur.
That sky, filled with the last colours of the day.
Ignore that smudge, sort it out tomorrow.
Someone else is waiting. Someone else is moving.
Not quite yet.
The green is not for me.
It's nearly time, but still I wait.

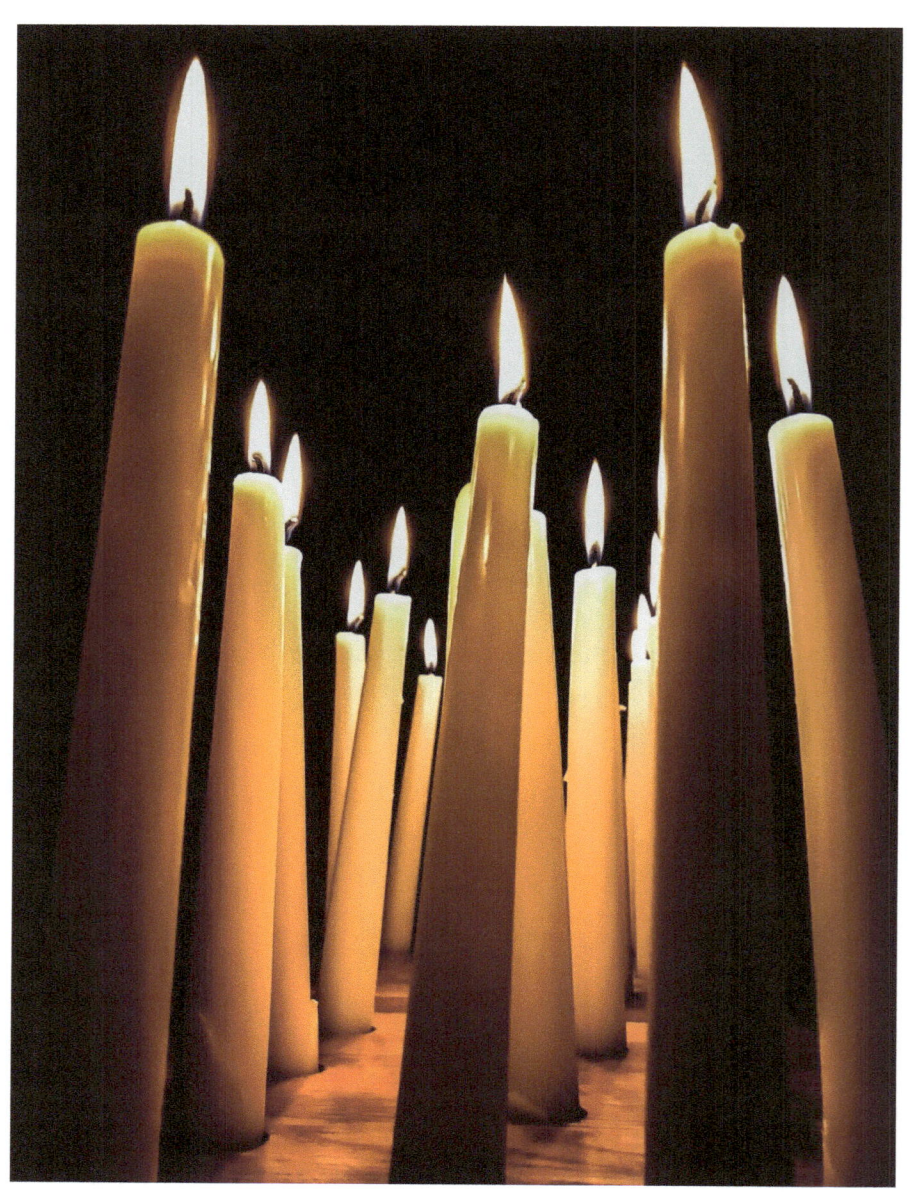

# ANTHONY SADLER-PUCKERING
## *JUST ONE CANDLE MORE*

A flick of light in the darkness
Something in the distance. I see
A shadow that looks upon us
If only the light would reach

I feel the presence within my space
But my voice is too small to speak
The thoughts in my mind are darker
But my face is the picture they see

Just one candle more could reach it
When I light one, it moves far from me
The strangest of places it goes to
But I follow it even if I can't breathe

The glow from the light is fading
Once the wick has burnt to a crisp
Let's hope the candles keep lighting
As the lighter no longer exists

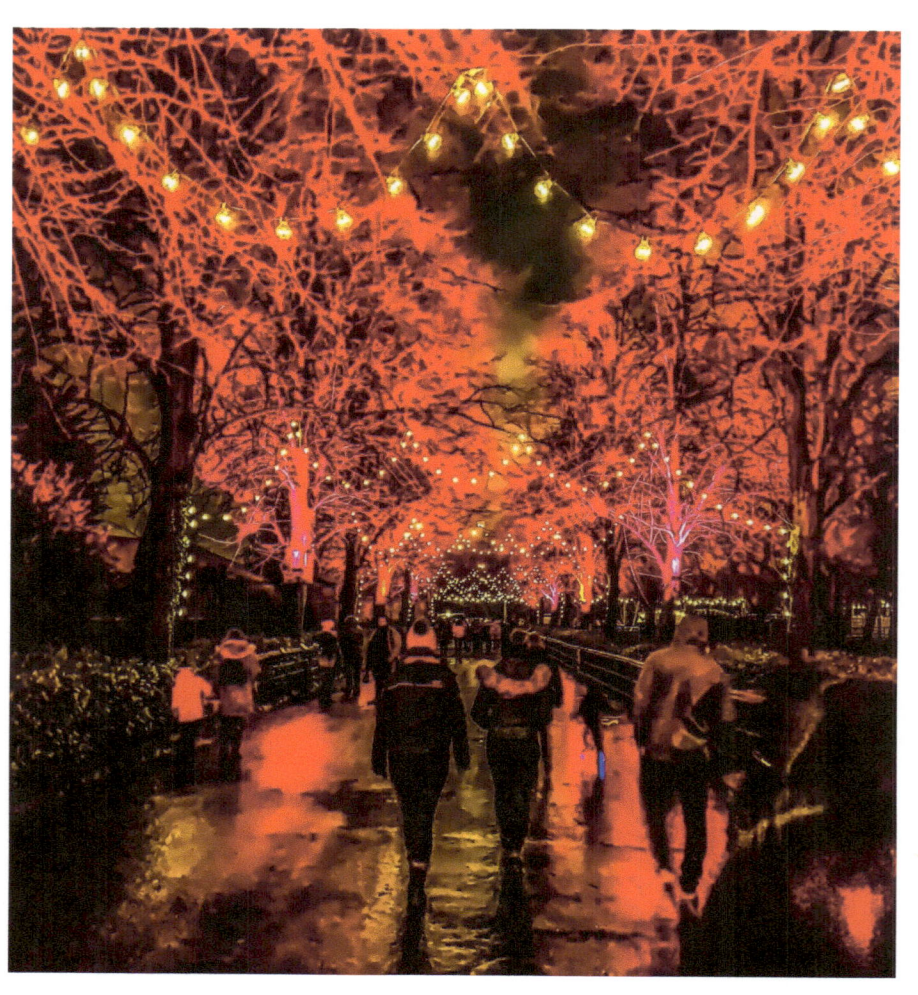

# MARIA BYRNE
## *SOMETIMES*

Sometimes Turner
And Lowry meet,
Across time.
The red autumnal colours
Merging, Morphing,
From the yellow
Of the summer.

And people.
Each into their own worlds,
The outside family life
The inner worlds of self,
The Winter wardrobe
Revolution.
Development,
Hoping for a winter
Resolve.

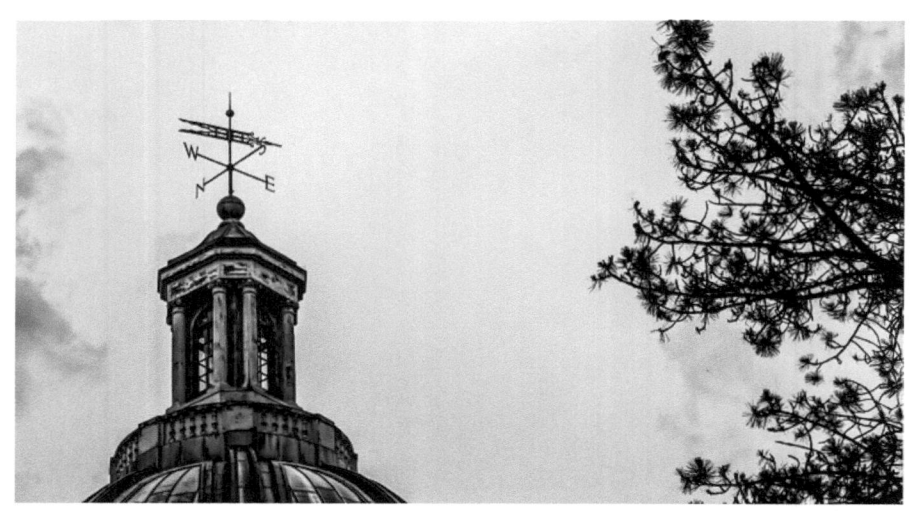

# JENNIFER TYSON
## *WINDS FROM THE EAST*

Winds from the East, there's a storm comin' in
Could this be our deliverance from sin?
Colonising slowly with pace to begin,
Then sweeping the world, it started to win.

Invisible, contagious, rapid and dangerous,
Mythical, fictional and by no means medical,
Contain it, avoid it, make space and control it.
Deny it, ignore it, protest and deplore it.

Friend of a friend of a friend infected.
Moving faster than we ever had expected.
Friend of a friend.
And now just a friend.
I cannot comprehend.
And now our resources are starting to expend.

The renegades deny and the rest of us, we cry:
separated, isolated, segregated.
And time and time again directed to live broadcasts,
Where rules are ceremoniously dictated.
And I hate it.

Smiles are obstructed and we cannot embrace,
This is honestly devastating to our love reliant, affection thriving, animalistic human race.
Protecting loved ones by staying apart,
But I need to be with them and it's breaking my heart.

Winds from the East, the storm came in.
This truly was our deliverance from sin.
Tentatively waiting for life to re - begin,
And we will never take it for granted, ever again.

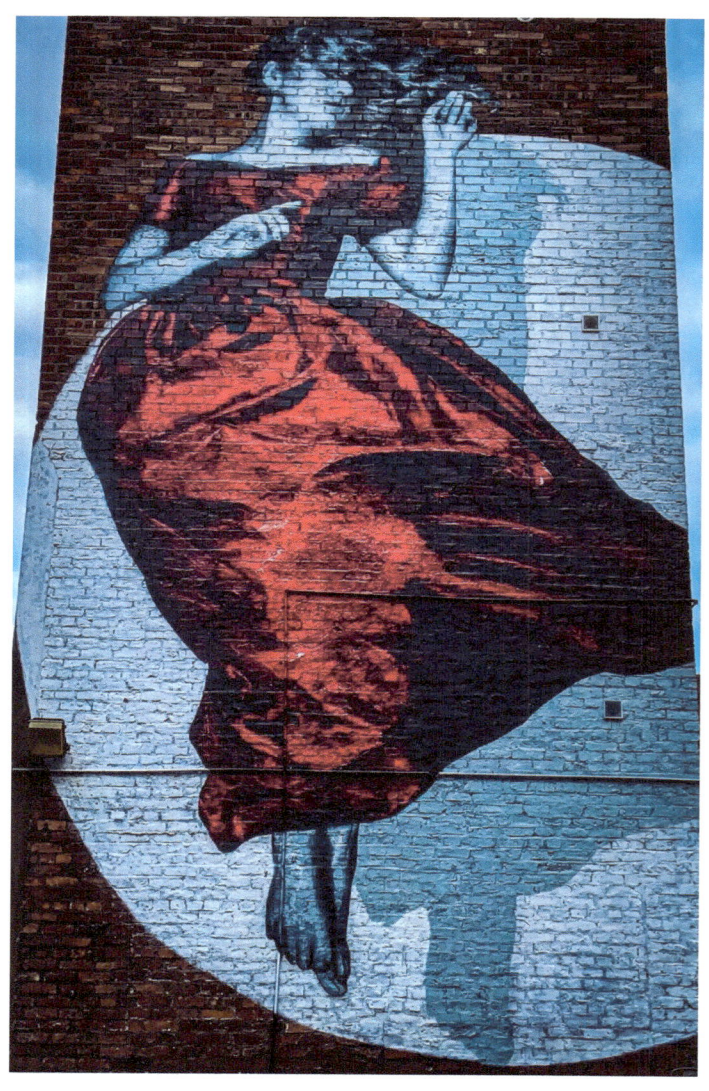

Background: The dramatic piece, named 'Serenity', comes courtesy of SNIK: a male-female duo who, with over a decade's experience, have established themselves as one of the most progressive stencil artists of the moment.

Of the piece (best seen from Lever Street), Cities of Hope said: "This tribute is in gratitude to all women that stand against injustice. The artwork recognises their strength, resolve and dignity; a testimony to what they have endured, and still endure, to make the world a better place for all of us."

# SARAH PRITCHARD

## *SERENITY*

By rights she should be in green & purple
For suffragette city
But I like the way
She took the romantic, sexy
dress of so many films
given by men to women
to stir THEIR passions
& instead wore it like
a menstrual flag...

We bled for you
We bleed for you
We keep bleeding for you
through the police batons &
gender biased courts to prison for
stealing to feed our babies
the seductive trapdoor of grooming & traffucking
the predatory streets of the red light zone
The loss of babies sun rise to sunset
The battering by partners
The gauntlet of rape culture media
In backstreets, behind you
In the grass roots of forgotten estates
We keep marching for justice
We stay rebel reddened
we float in our blood red frock
buoyed up by mother moon.

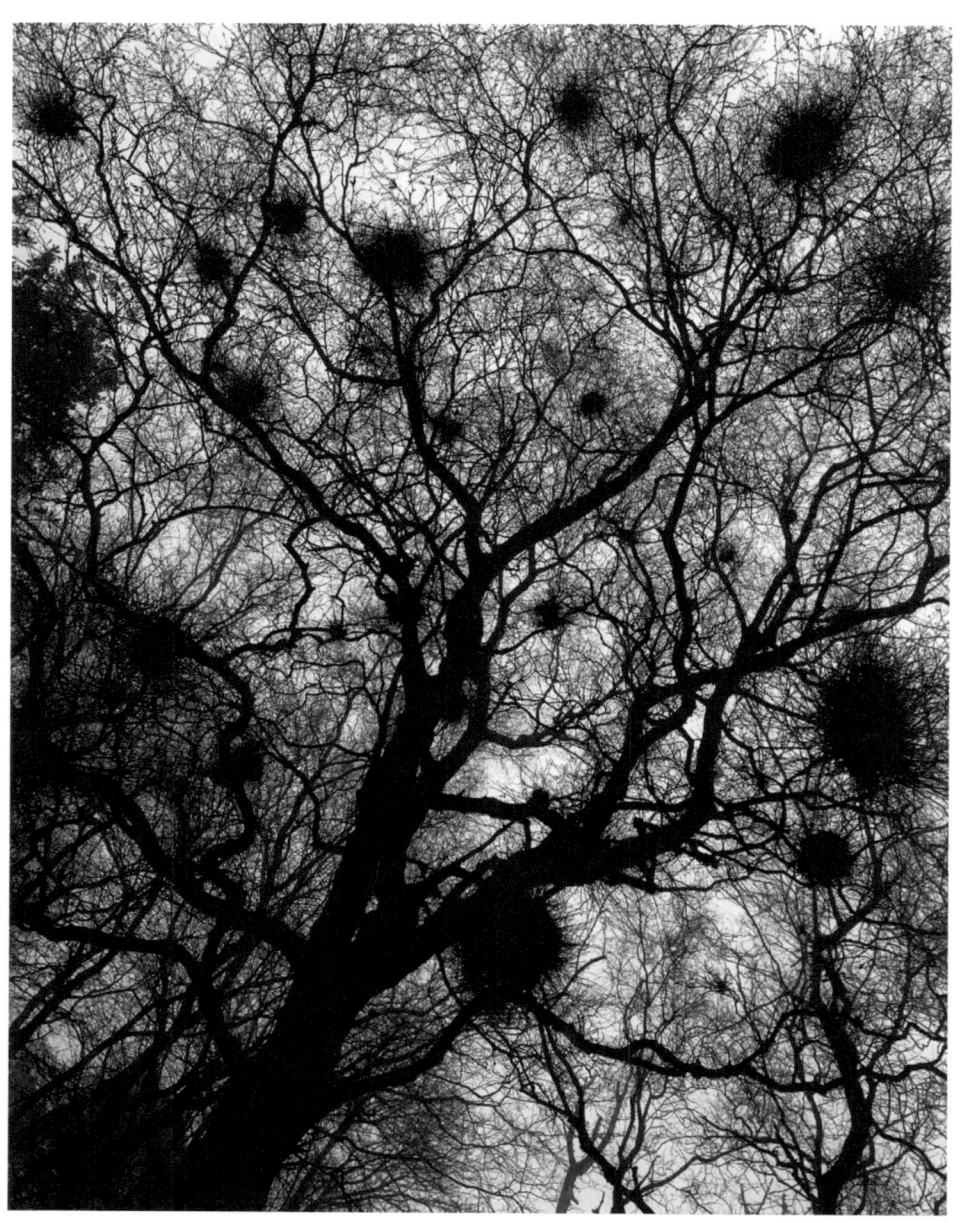

# EMMA HULANCE
## *BLACK BERETS*

Black berets
Hooked on tendrils of tree
Whilst owners ride free
Flowing hair liberation.
Streaks of silver burning bright
Stars catch light on split ends
High over mountain and moon.

And all this by day coiled inside a bun inside a hat.

Shapeshifting is a myth.
Bewitching is in the eye of the beholder.

The hats are gone by daylight break.
The tree stands empty again -
Just black arteries against the gaunt sky:
A witches empty locker room
Containing all the secrets.

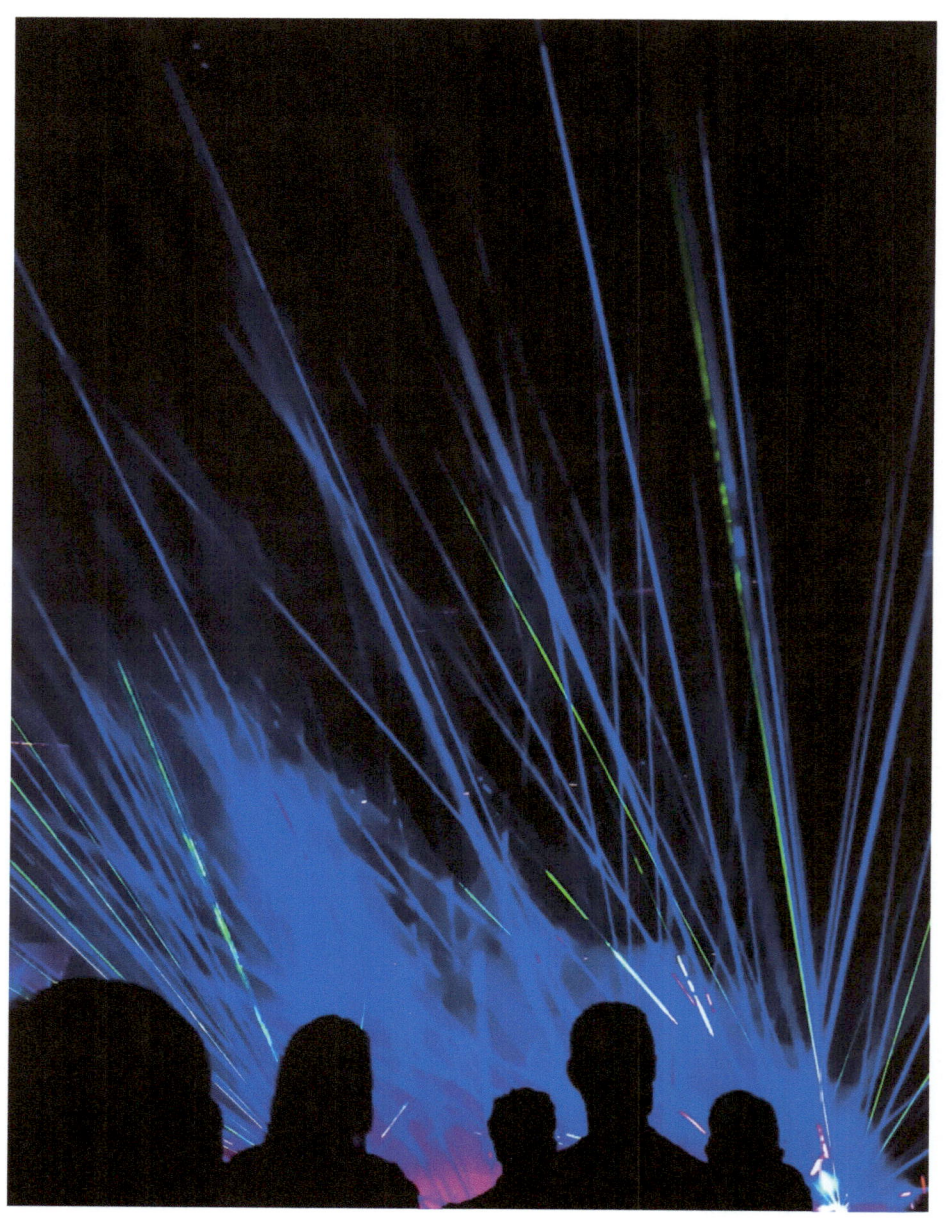

# JOEL SADLER-PUCKERING
*THEY BUILT THIS PLACE*

Beneath a black sea
of our hopelessness
and our despair
we hide beneath the
laser beams of the rainbow.
Here in this moment
the neon cuts through our pain
and slices it into bitesize pieces
    - we swallow it whole.

Baselines throb against
the red brickwork and
silence the lingering whispers
of the subjugated underpaid workers
who couldn't feed their children.
They built this place.
Although we are still shackled
in many ways, Gospel-tinged
lyrics preach to us about freedom.

But we do not pray on this night.

We are euphoric, holding
our hands high in the air
suspended beneath the rainbow of light
and in anticipation for better days.

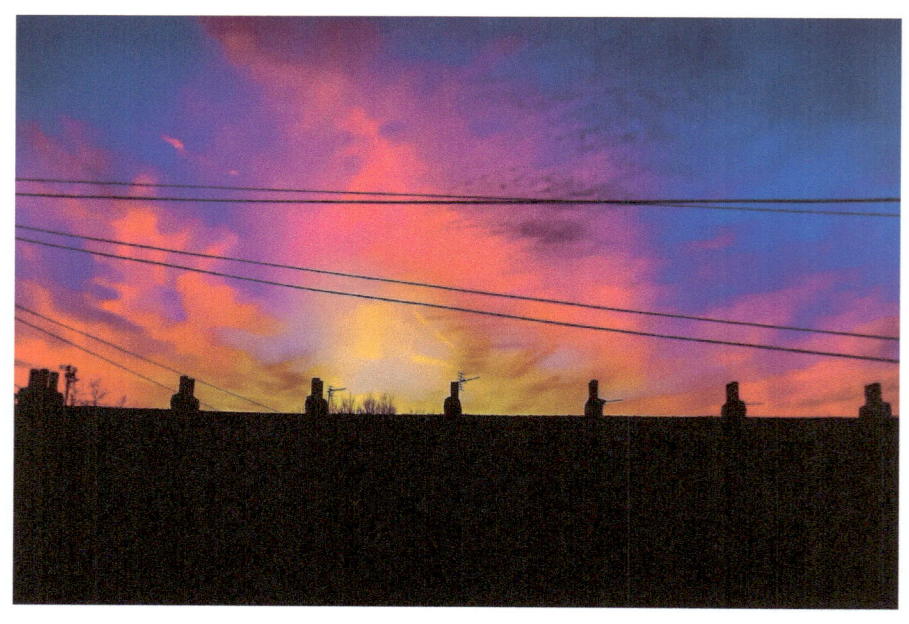

# KATIE HAIGH
## *PAINTINGS BY NATURE*

Fire burns the sky,
Over roof tops.
Slates glisten,
With nature's fireworks.
Colours burst.
Yellows, reds, oranges and purples,
On a canvas of deepening blue.
A symphony for the eyes.
Soothing for the soul.
Lighting up faces,
That cannot help but smile,
At nature's magnificent beauty.

©K.Haigh

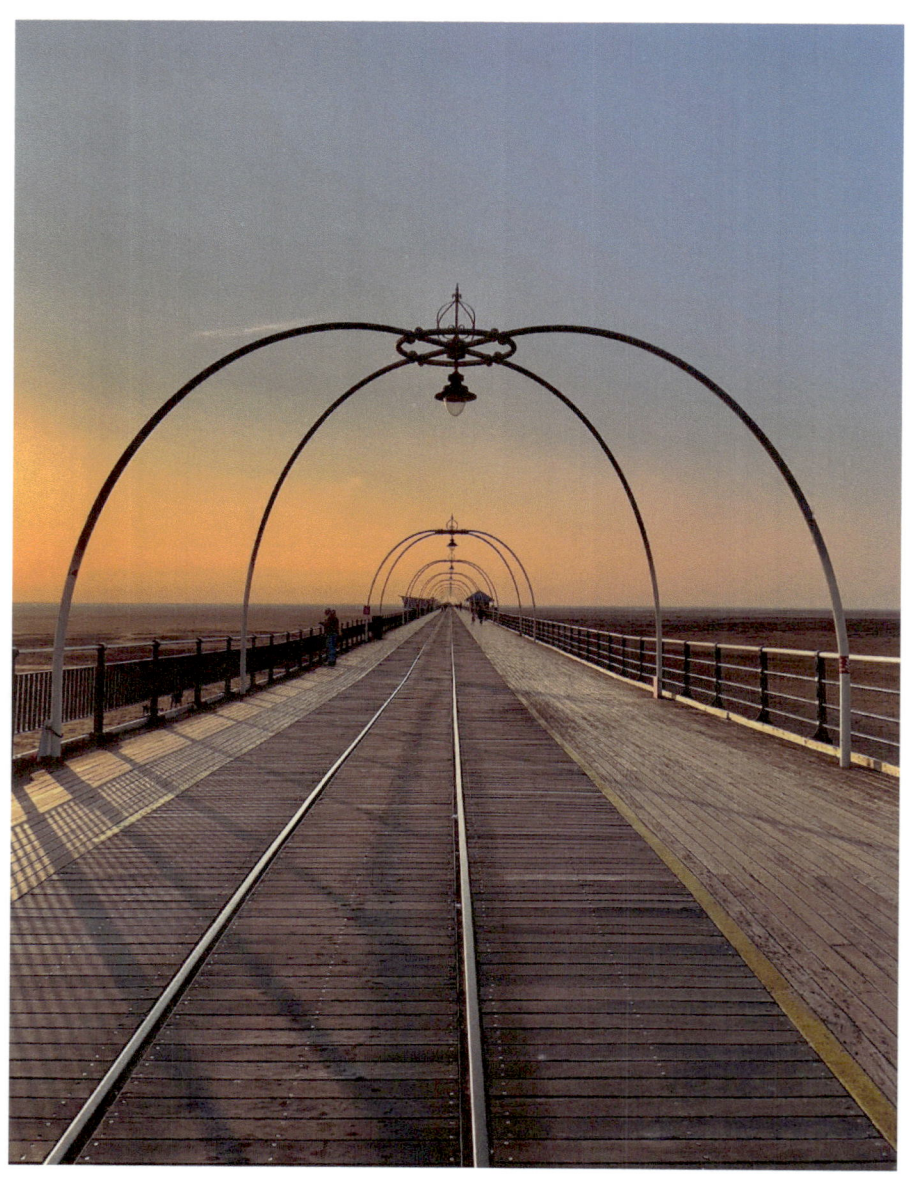

# CAROLYNNE NELSON
## *IT WON'T BE FOREVER*

When I go, it won't be forever
You'll see me there over the shoreline
I'll wave and make you smile.
My lips on your cheek you'll remember softly.
Many nights we spent there,
On the shore.
In embrace, chasing the stars
laughing away.

When you go, it won't be forever.
We'll be together like always.

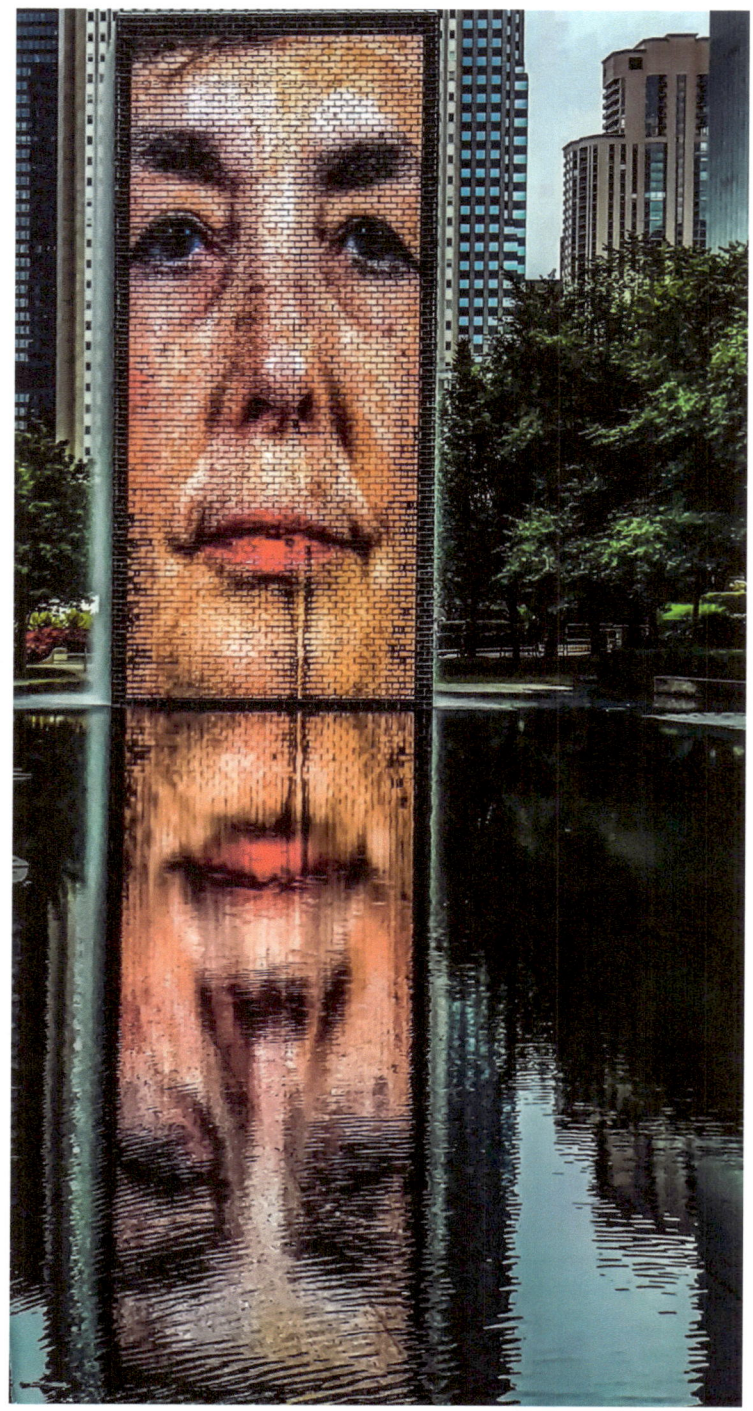

# BOUND IMAGER
*PAUL JAMES CULSHAW*

Sliding reflection, immortally trapped.
Stained in the urban life,
using patches of colour to attract.
They draw us in closer.
We become intrigued.
Watching. Hour by hour.
They see everything - maybe just what they need.

Who else comes to visit them?
We are all strangers at first sight.
How long do we stay together?
We don't stop to think, we just follow the bright light.
Unknowingly we become connected.
They see us for who we are, in the long dark night.

Never on their own, they are two of the same
Upside down they can see everything, which one is to blame?
Distorted like a damaged oil painting.
Vacantly viewing, no emotions for us to feel.
Never knowing their story, but we're all part of that deal.

In our moments together we can pretend.
Time stays with them right to the end.
There's so much that we never say.
Sometimes, we just walk away.
But the face, looks on.
Always the same.

## *HIDDEN VOICE PUBLISHING*

Hidden Voice Publishing is an independent publishing resource centre that supports & represents authors from under-represented groups with publishing paperback and Amazon Kindle books.

## TITLES ON HIDDEN VOICE PUBLISHING

*I KNOW WHY THE GAY MAN DANCES*
*JOEL SADLER-PUCKERING*

*INKY BLACK WOMAN*
*MINA AIDOO*

*FERAL ANIMALS*
*JOEL SADLER-PUCKERING*

*WHEN WOMEN FLY*
*SARAH PRITCHARD*

*HIDDEN VOICE ANTHOLOGY: VOLUME 1*
*VARIOUS AUTHORS*

# TITLES ON HIDDEN VOICE PUBLISHING

*HIDDEN VOICE ANTHOLOGY: VOLUME 2*
*VARIOUS AUTHORS*

*TEN POEMS FOR PRIDE*
*SARAH PRITCHARD & JOEL SADLER*

*BOY(ISH) VEST*
*CARSON WOLFE*

*TAKING BACK MY RAINBOW*
*JOEL SADLER-PUCKERING*

*AND NO ONE HEARD HER CRIES*
*PAULINE OMOBOYE*

*TELL ME WHAT YOU SEE*
*PAUL JAMES CULSHAW*

www.ingramcontent.com/pod-product-compliance
Lightning Source LLC
Chambersburg PA
CBHW040258220526
45473CB00002B/522